First published in Great Britain, 1993 by
The Bodley Head Children's Books
an imprint of Random House UK Limited
20 Vauxhall Bridge Road
London SW1V 2SA

Random House Australia (Pty) Limited
20 Alfred Street, Milsons Point, Sydney,
New South Wales 2061, Australia

Random House New Zealand Limited
18 Poland Road, Glenfield, Auckland 10,
New Zealand

Random House South Africa (Pty) Limited
PO Box 337, Bergvlei, 2012, South Africa

Set in Pilgrim Roman by Creative Text Limited
Printed and bound in Hong Kong

A catalogue record for this book is
available from the British Library

ISBN 0 370 318 056

THE SNOW ANGEL

Angela McAllister
Illustrated by Claire Fletcher

THE BODLEY HEAD
London

It was the first snow morning. Elsa made giant's footsteps to the frozen dewpond. She built snow castles, and she slid down the slippery slope.

Then she found a secret place. Elsa lay on the snow blanket and spread her arms like wings. She made the shape of an angel.

Elsa showed her friend Jack. 'This is where a snow angel lay,' she whispered. That Jack always thought her tales were true.

'I wish I could see a snow angel,' he sighed, 'more than anything in the whole wide world.'

The next morning Jack found Elsa. He was very excited.

'I saw her! I saw the snow angel last night, sweeping away the snowdrifts. And she gave me a wish and I rode the big rabbit. And it's true, I really did.' But Elsa just smiled. That Jack was always dreaming.

The next morning Jack looked everywhere for Elsa.

'The snow angel came again!' he said. 'She melted the ice with her breath. And she gave me a wish, and all the fish were flying fish, even that old whiskery. And I saw it, I really saw it.' But Elsa just smiled. That Jack was always telling stories.

The next morning Jack was waiting for Elsa.

'The swinging tree was so heavy with snow it was going to crash through the window, and the snow angel blew it all away. And she gave me a wish and all the icicles were made of sugar. And I ate one hundred and I really, really did.' But Elsa just smiled. That Jack was a good pretender.

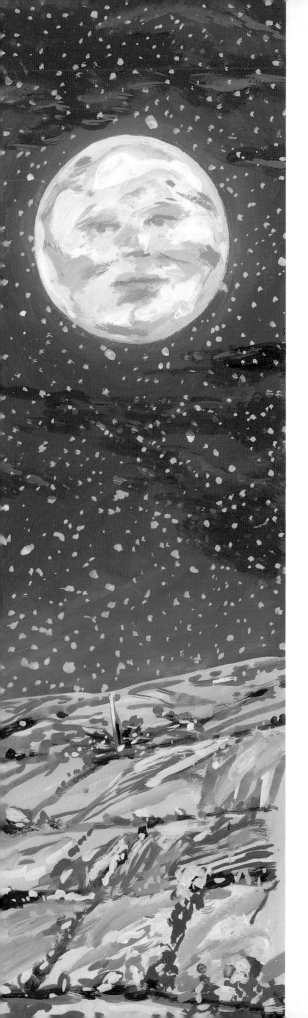

That night a fresh snow fall covered the giant's footsteps and the castles and the slippery slope. Everything was buried deep. But, when Elsa returned to the secret place, an angel's shape still glistened in the snow. Were those the wings she had made?

Gently Elsa lay down. She thought about Jack. She shut her eyes and made a wish. And when she sat up the snow wings began to grow.

First little snow buds, then long soft, white feathers unfolded and lifted her high amongst the trees!

Up and up and Elsa flew through the frosty air. She shook the branches, she stood on the treetops, she skimmed the stepping stream. Then low among the trees someone was hiding.

And Elsa flew.

All morning she flew with the snow angel in and out of the blue shadows, until the sun began to melt her wings. One last swoop over the church spire then softly Elsa fell to earth.

Jack met Elsa at the slippery slope. He was very excited. 'I didn't see a snow angel this morning . . . I saw two!'

Elsa looked up through the snowflakes and laughed. Maybe that Jack knew a true thing after all. 'Come on then Jack,' she said, 'let's make giant's footsteps in this snow.'